STREWTH

HOW to BE

an **AUSSIE**

in 10 MINUTES!!!

All the Words, Sayings and Aussie Stuff

to Fill YOUR Boots!

By Bill 'Scratch' Cunningham

Disclaimer

STREWTH!!

HOW to Be

An AUSSIE

in 10 Minutes!!!

CONTENTS

1.   p17 ... AUSTRALIA – Warts and ALL

A Short History: Cuisine. Fashion. Hairstyles. Sport. Arts and Crafts. Identities. Humour. Common Chatter.

2.   P31... The Lingo – Everyday Australian Words

3.   P63... WHOA Slow Down ... Modern Trends

4.   P69 ... HOW to Speak like an AUSSIE -

includes 12 EASY Ways!

5.   P83 ... Conclusion ...

The SUN Sets in the Outback

Books by Bill 'Scratch' Cunningham

About the Author

References

STREWTH

STONE THE CROWS!

What's the go with Oz?

People just don't get it.

Are you the same?

Do you struggle to get your head around the Australian way of doing things and moreover the way they actually say things?

Well cobber, settle down. You just need to grab a sanga or sausage sizzle, wash it down with some neck oil and chillax. It's no use rushing on the tucker as you don't want to chunder. And remember to go easy on the three cheers you don't want to look like a wally if you over indulge.

Firstly, to understand a little bit of the why and what for of the Aussie way of doing things you probably need to consider some relaxation time. So, here's an idea ... why not now head down to the beach to watch the world go by? But watch=out for the after darks! It will probably be a 'beaut' arvo with an optic never or two as the good bodies walk on by. Don't forget your thongs it's Summer and it's hot out.

Blokes don't forget the budgie smugglers. Now, lay out the farmer's plough and take it all in.

You know, up the line they don't get much time to do this but when they get a chance to hit the big smoke their brains run amok looking at what city folk get up to.

Unless you have a few kangaroos loose in the top paddock there is no way you wouldn't enjoy down under with all the scenery (and the beach is just one type). There's heap more. Hit the frog and toad, go out west, or hit the bush and simply people watch, take in some adventures and abuse the climate ... and you can't lose.

But hold onto your nuts. You will soon realise that Australians are unique. Although you may encounter a few bogans and tall poppy's overall the chance to blend in with people from ambos and garbos to musos and poli's will delight you especially when you realise there's a whole new world out there (right-here) and full of colourful language to boot. But hold on don't spit the dummy with what lay ahead, please don't go off like frog in a sock. Fair dinkum it's not an insurmountable task to take it all in. You have plenty of time to learn the lingo and understand the Australian way of life!

So, what I'm saying is give me just some of your reason and rhyme and we can solve the dilemma.

Get it?

Got it?

No?

Ah ... Well ... Good!

Now, YOU MAY NOT KNOW WHAT ALL THIS MEANS BUT, I guarantee BY THE END OF THIS BOOK YOU WILL!

And you will learn just a little about what makes the average Aussie tick just for shits and giggles as well!!

So, let's get started!

The Australian

Australians are as unique as they come. From their social sense, habits and vernacular there is quite possibly no other distinctive race on earth that has you commonly scratching your head to work out who they are, what they mean and whether they are the full quid (have any sense at all). Or perhaps many simply believe them to be a work of art 'in progress'. Any way you look at it most Aussies like to believe they are warm, giving and friendly.

Along with their ability to evenly flow between boardroom suits to tradie wear, tank tops, boardies and thongs (flip=flops); switching from elegant evening /social attire to trackie dacks (tracksuit pants) and sloppy joes (pullovers) they can mingle with best as they manage to 'scoff' down bangers (sausages), smash some mash (potato mash), burgers and bickies (cookies) whilst polishing off (drinking) coldies or indeed imbibing in champers and caviar. This is possibly amidst a maddening crowd joking around at a barbie (BBQ), in the surf, during a high social tea or even banging the bush (trekking in the countryside).

You know, the average Aussie maybe garbos (garbage removalists), coppers (police), posties(post deliverers), ambos (ambulance/paramedics), merchant bankers, health practitioners, artists and sportspeople that would assimilate in any crowd and once you can effectively mingle with then even query out loud our pollies (politicians) and argue about climate change with the best of them then you can understand the average Aussie a little better. Following on from this once you can learn to effectively 'veg out' (hold a vegetative state of mind) when things become a little chaotic, surf, swim, drive some cattle , shear a sheep or even just chill and chat on your smarties (smart phones) in a fluent 'matter of course' way then congrats you are nearly some way more to understanding the Aussie . But, this aside perhaps it is only when you truly master the lingo that you can really call yourself an honorary Aussie ... and the last bit is the easiest bit (with a little practice of course!)

Most Aussie aren't singularly distinctive rather what you experience or hear may not be totally remarkable to the Australian way because there are plenty of overlays with British humour and American=isms; a combination which adds to understanding part of the Australian identity. For instance, dress sense = Aussie style is probably as common around the globe as are most food and drink choices nowadays. There is however, a rather distinct feature amongst our western culture folk of Europe and the Americas and that is most of our address i.e. communication with more than 4000-

word choices recorded in our wordbook, uses more short or trimmed words than any other common European or Asian countries. Aussie love to play with words besides other things. We often clip things just for the sake of it and when you truly analyse it often its unnecessary. Researchers call this shortening of words 'diminutives'.

So along with a quick blast of Aussie culture, along with some colloquialisms and Aussie ways here is a collective of Aussie-isms or simply put How to be an Aussie in 10 minutes!

If your next trip is to the land Down Under or you want to play catch up with what is going on in Oz (Australia) or if you simply dig Australian isms, the following introduces you to a taste of some of our favourite fashions, foods and most of all sayings. And even if you have visited these shores before you may just be able to add a few quips, tips and words to your arsenal of knowledge and Aussie know-how just through browsing this booklet.

BUT REMEMBER... Just take a chunk of seriousness out of the equation. You see, Aussies like to keep it all light- hearted. They have their own way of seeing and doing things.

But I'm jumping the gun a bit so let's take a step back...

1

Australia – WARTS and ALL

A Brief History

Australia is a self-governing country but serves under the Commonwealth of countries with the Queen of England as its reigning monarchy. It is comprised of the mainland of the Australian continent, the island of Tasmania and numerous small islands. It was first inhabited by indigenous Australians for about 50 000 years plus before the first white settlement in the late 18th century. abc

According to all the geography books, Australia's land mass of some 7.6 million square kilometres gives rise to a plethora of landscapes including centre deserts, rain forest up the north and mountains down south=east. It is steeped in an eclectic array of country side. abc

Australia is highly developed country with the Worlds' 14th largest economy, has an extensive telecommunications network exports, is rich in resources including coal, iron ore and is underpinned by a strong banking, finance, search and rescue and services base.

Australia is made up of various cultures with ancestries dominant not only in England 30% but infused with German, Italian, Greek and even Dutch influence the latter roughly over 1 %. Notably, the indigenous population makes up 2.8% of the population* (at last count of the 2016 National census).abc

Cuisine

Most indigenous Australian tribal groups subsist on a simple hunter gatherer type diet of native flora and fauna called bush tucker whilst multicultural Australia transformed the local dinner plate from meat and 3 veg in the 40's and 50's into a smorgasbord of fine and eclectic array of European Mediterranean and Asian delights especially post WW2. The coffee culture in Oz is amongst the strongest and best in the world. A colloquial amount of traditional food and beverage types exist with names bandied around to make them sound more distinctive for examples:

'Sausage Sizzle' = an event for friends, charity or fund raising at which butchers' sausages are post BBQ and slapped between two pieces of bread with a few onions thrown in.

Pav = the traditional cake of pavlova.

Damper = traditional great tasting bread common in bakeries.

'Lamington Drive' = a charity drive starring packets of Lamingtons.

'Mugaccino' = a cappuccino in a mug.

Sanga (er) = a sandwich.

A dog's eye i.e. = a meat or chicken pie; a delight wrapped in thick pastry.

Vegemite = a yeast extract spread on bread / toast (a particular taste!)

A cat's eye = sausage roll; meat packet cylindrical covered with pastry.

Australian beer is held in high world regard along with locally produced wine grown mainly in the southern cooler parts of the country.

But, 2019 sees most of Australia cater for all food and drink types with its non-discriminating multiculturalism effecting one of the most different and understanding mixes in the world today.

Fashion

Australians love a challenge when it comes to fashion. Although lagging some 6 months behind our European and American counterparts they do appreciate and indulge in the best there is when available. That stated they are susceptible to holding on a bit longer than is necessarily see Velcro wallets, fluoro hyper=colour (you know the changing colour t-shirt, undies, socks and shorts), leggings, sweat bands, anything Farah Fawcett-Majors (just joking here), Star Wars and Hawaiian shirts! Still they hold onto budgie smugglers (men's' swimming briefs) for good reason! Fashion labels from the likes of Akira Isogawa, Colette Dinnigan, Lisa Ho, Chris Chronis and Fred Fox compete with the world's best.

If one is to attire fittingly then a little tending to detail is called for. For instance, a pair of swimming bathers are called cossies, swimming togs or bathers whereas budgie smugglers are really swimming briefs for men (NOT surfing board shorts).

Women: If you want to get fair dinkum (real), Australian women generally prefer a pair of dressy shorts with wedges. You can as female choose denim off cuts and rubber flip flops (thongs) for city use or out and about. Use some sneakers or runners for sightseeing even some loafers. Light weight material in summer and spring is good especially re shorts whilst rugging up for a moderate Winter (see jeans, jumper and runners) will see you out for sightseeing.

Mostly women love to dress well and be healthy like most females world-wide. The city-sides are usually full of athletic joggers, all-aged walkers, swimmers, early morning gym goers or early risers who may indulge sensible summer glow or a smoothie in winter.

For the night out women wear heels and look the part like in minor cocktail party attire somewhat downsized. Swap out most of the shorts for jeans or pants in the winter matched with a nice blouse or t=shirts and cardigans or simple layered wear.

Additionally, low cut boots are always in mode as are short skirts complimented with long sleeves. Don't forget to throw in a ripping party dress and a pair of heels for city night life.

The outback and Bush are well known for it's a pub atmosphere detailed with jeans, boots and a flannelette shirt with hat or night-time jeans and shirt or polo top finished with a layered top.

Aussies in the deep throes of sunshine i.e. at the top end (the Northern Territory of Australia) live in things like t-shirts, tank tops and shorts (consider cotton for breathing) as it can get unevenly sweltering at times. Scuffs, flip- flops and sandals work best for foot attire as enclosed foot wear can be most uncomfortable.

Men: For men beach clobber includes boardies (board-shorts) any type of short and t-shirt. If you are invited to a picnic then consider nice shorts, shirt or a polo shirt whilst boat shoes or loafers do the job for the feet.

Night life includes an array of choices: Cool t-shirts, shirts and jeans/pants, nice shoes, boots or fancy designer lace-ups.

Overall, the amount of clothing to bring or use should correspond with the type of situation you will find yourself in. There is no one fits all dress code due to the wide ranges in temperatures and social settings. So, dress according to what's in store ... (you know long socks and sandals went out quite a while, ago don't you?)

Hairstyles

Women salons and hairstyles are up to speed with the latest fashion cuts courtesy of social media, internet and of course magazines. In 2019, the hair styles for men include the Clooney look (a George Clooney side hair part). For the last 6 years or so the short haircut, with the bushranger beard (which now seems to be 'completed' by some form of upper body tattoo) holds sway for a particular type of male. Regarding tattoos, the women aren't far behind though some aren't into growing beards yet!

Sport

Australia is bred on sport and according to well-placed sources at Wiki at last count over 24% of Australians past 15 years of age participated in organised sports activities. [256]

Australia loves anything sporty but are imbued mainly with a spirited passion for football in the Winter: Rugby league, rugby Union, Soccer and AFL for both genders whilst Netball for women has its many devotees. In the summer months outside beaches and BBQ there is a passion for softball, touch football, summer soccer and athletics. Aussies also thrive on outback trekking, bush walking, adventure trails, jogging and basketball whilst they have produced world champion wood choppers, shearers and drovers which sit equally alongside the many who partake in a fervent beach scene; world leading in both surfing and lifesaving.

Aussies stop for Australia day January 26 (white settlement), Anzac day in April 25 (commemorating soldiers who have fought in the wars), Easter, labour day (commemorating working rights), the Queen's birthday in June, and a particular horse race called the Melbourne cup held in November each year (pens down, stop work, forget whatever you are doing, grab some food and drink, catch a horse from an office sweep and watch 3 minutes of one of the world's most prestigious races) whilst a race of another kind the Sydney to Hobart yacht race takes place each boxing Day. Both hold collective sway over the nation outside of election time (and that is another story of polly (politicians) and people deciding who best fits the shoe this time!) And then, there is Christmas and end of season celebrations!!!

Australian Arts and crafts

Australian arts and crafts have been dominated over the years by a wide range of contributors who have helped shape Australia's place on the world art and craft map and they include but not limited to:

Pro Hart, Sydney Nolan and Norman Lindsay have helped establish a modernistic mainstream art acceptance whilst indigenous artists Namatjira, Emily Kame Kngwarreye and Mminnie Pwerle became powerful indigenous figures in contemporary indigenous art. In fact, Indigenous rock art is the oldest and abundant in the world dating as far back as 50 000 years plus and outspread across innumerable sites.

Aussie Identities

Sure, I have probably left out a few notable identities but by and by the following have made some sort of dent nurturing the Aussie way of life:

Amongst the earliest pioneers was Mat Flinders explorer and navigator; the first man to navigate the continent as well as giving Australia its name.

Captain James Cook controversially, the first white man to step foot and settle on indigenous land in 1770.

Inventor and engineer = John Bradford.

Sydney Opera House Architect = Jorn Utzon.

Medicine people like Howard Florey who worked on the introduction of Penicillin and Dr Elizabeth Blackburn winner of the Nobel prize for her work in genetics.

Sir Edmund Barton = Australia's first Prime Minister.

Daisy Bates = social worker.

Eddie Mabo = social rights for indigenous people.

Peter Carey= literature.

Adam Goodes = former champion AFL player and champion of human and indigenous rights.

Les Murray = poet.

Mandawup Yunupingu = musician.

Neville Bonner = first aboriginal parliamentarian.

Cathy Freeman = champion athlete.

Yvonne Goolagong =tennis champion.

Mick Dodson = professor of law.

A.B 'Banjo' Patterson = who not only revered Australia in poetry but his literature skills and managerial achievement helped bloom the country worldwide.

Morris West = novelist.

Pat White = Australia's only Nobel prize winner in literature David Williamson = playwright.

Dame Joan Sutherland = operatic singer.

Peter Thompson = champion golfer.

Shane Warne = cricketer.

Phar Lap and Winx = champion world racehorses.

Sir Donald Bradman = cricketer; recognised as one the greatest 10 sportspeople to have ever lived.

Nancy Wake = the 'white-mouse' resistance fighter during the war years.

Kylie Minogue = entertainer.

Mel Gibson = actor.

Errol Flynn = actor.

Robert Hawke = Prime Minister.

Saint Mary Mackillop = religious order.

Oodgeroo Noonuccle = writer and activist.

... and so many more have contributed to making Australia what it is today.

Humour

Australians have a strong relationship with self-=humour and perhaps this is one of the main reasons why they are so hardy. They constantly choose to make fun of themselves. Completing tasks without the usual intermittent jibe or joke is well accepted although world-wide political correctness still rules.

Often the more undignified the nickname, the better.

Self-deprecation is commonly abounding and for good reason. Perhaps the Monty Python-*esque* humour rubs off on Aussies unintended but never the less helps to nurture an Aussie who never takes them self too seriously.

The Aussie has the opinion that everyone has his/her rightful place although inevitably is expendable and so with good reason makes sure that seriousness has its place and time but so to do good doses of laughter and reality checks. Friends are easy to come by if you know how to use nicknames, banter easily with average Aussie colloquialisms and just listen without getting or giving a migraine! If you can down play the gravity in normal situations then the locals find it endearing. Sarcasm helps... within reason!

Common chatter

What's in at the moment?

If people are discussing housing construction, working conditions, hospitals or road networks, cost of groceries, cost of utilities; electricity, gas and water then you could be anywhere in the world but here, it is common for people to discuss the above and a tad more.

It is common for people to live at home until their late 20s, and house sharing is common even for people into their mid to late 30's. Single accommodation say in a bed-sitter or one bedroom apartment will take a huge chunk out of your wage but even though you can't afford the luxuries in life, you can often cheat and look like you can. A couple of nice couches (sofas), boutique beers in the fridge and some well-placed lamingtons help to cope a bit better.

Make sure you don't forget to abuse the weather and complain about the government. Then if you learn to snap chat, Instagram, tweet and stamp your place in the Aussie smart phone world effectively throwing in a few philosophical statements on social media as well then slowly you migrate to the Aussie way of doing things!

On top of this, once you mention farm animals and New Zealand in the same conversation, if you can say G'day in the city and really mean have a 'good day', respect indigenous people (they do not like being photographed without permission. They are not an oddity but at last starting to be respected for who they are and their values), feel free enough to use 'no worries', 'ta' (thanks), 'arvo' (afternoon), and 'brekkie', abuse the weather again, complain heaps about the government then you are accumulating the 'I'm an Aussie' patches to be worn invisibly upon your chest.

Additionally, if you create some bias in your state local conversation for example if you live in Sydney, you hate Melbourne and if you live in Melbourne, you hate Sydney or nationally you understand the Aussie v everyone else with notable mention to the kiwis (New Zealanders) and septic tanks (yanks or Americans) and poms (English) the metamorphoses to being Australian continues strongly. Now, if you proceed to remain laid back in all circumstances even when you are being ridiculed or held accountable for just or unjust reasons, sprinkle the truth with dust of far-fetched statements or better still humour then along with all the slang and funny words you are DEFINITELY on your way to being an honorary Australian.

2

The lingo!

Average everyday Australian words

Australians are well known for their use or abuse of the English language. And perhaps that is the hardest thing for a tourist or new Australian to get their head around...the Aussie's command of the English language.

The average Aussie vernacular contains an innumerable variety of cut words, slang terms and colloquialisms used on an everyday basis. For those on holidays or joining the ranks of Down-under on a full-time basis these terms may take some learning, understanding and indeed justifying.

Australians speak differently than most nationalities including Americans and the British. The reason for this is when the Brits colonised the joint the British accent was most prominent, but over time the generations coming through developed a new localised accent. Considering the bulk of 'new' Australians were convicts it comes as no surprise that few P's and IQ's went missing in the vocabulary. It is also believed that, due to immigration, the South England and Southeast Asian accents and lately European (the last 50 years) and recent American influence through social media have had a lot of influence over the modern-day Australian accent mixing pronunciation, inflection and delivery in new found adapted ways.

And so, the Aussie voice was adapted to its place and time although not all Australians speak with a twang and leave words uncompleted!

Over time the accent and word use has continued to evolve but still the basic Aussie language underpins any hew hybrid language and word use which is used in the 21st century. That written, here we go. This is what you need to know to get it together when someone says the following:

A

Aggro = aggressive.

Amber fluid = beer.

Ant's pants = height of fashion, or to think highly of yourself.

Arvo = afternoon.

Aussie = Australian.

Ay = pardon me.

A cold one = beer.

Accadacca = rock band Ac/ Dc.

Ankle biter = young child.

'Avva good weeken' = have a good weekend.

Use: Did you avva good weeken'?

After darks = rhyming slang for sharks.

Aussie salute = the act of brushing blowflies from one's face.

As crook as Rookwood = seriously ill. 'Crook' being actually sick, like at death's door, and Rookwood once being the biggest graveyard in Australia.

Arvo/arvi = afternoon. Use: 'Have a good arvo' or 'see you this arvo'.

'Aye, don't come the raw prawn' = STOP talking shit.

'av' a go ya mug'= come on get into whatever you are doing. For example, in sports or even at work. Use: at a cricket match when the scoring is slow = 'av a go ya mug' to speed things up!

'As useful as an ashtray on a motorbike' = honesty with explaining how you find someone who is helping you and they really are not.

Avo = avocado.

B

Bail = to cancel plans. Use: 'I'm bailing out.'

Bloke = male.

Bloody oath = the truth. Use: 'Yes, bloody oath he did it.'

Bruce = Aussie bloke.

Back o'Bourke = back of out-there, beyond, middle of absolutely nowhere.

Barbie = barbecue.

Barking up the wrong tree = just completely off the intended meaning or struggling with a misapprehension.

Barrack = cheerfulness at sporting event, supporting your side.

Battler = struggler and never gives up under turmoil.

Beanie = warm winter headcap, ski hat.

Beat around the bush = evading the point of the matter in a conversation.

Bewdie = unreal, great.

Belt up = stop talking!

Better half = husband or wife or partner.

Bikey = motor cyclist.

Billabong = water hole in dried=up river bed.

Billy = tin flask or vessel used to boil tea in the bush.

Biscuit = cookie.

Block = get angry. Use: 'I've done my block.'

Bloke = man.

Blower = telephone. Use: 'I'm just on the blower.'

Blowies = blow flies.

Bludge = do nothing.

Bludger = lazy person and who want participate; one who won't work.

Bluey = swag, nickname for a red=haired person.

Bonzer = great!

Boogie board = half the size of a surf board used to body surf.

Boomer = very big, large male kangaroo.

Boomerang = bowed smooth wooden utensil used by Aborigines for pursuing game.

Booze = alcohol.

Booze bus = police truck / van used for picking out people who may be alcohol induced as they drive their car.

Bottle shop = liquor shop.

Brekkie = breakfast.

Brown=eye = to reveal one's ring or bottom.

Buckley's = no chance at all.

Bung on = put on.

Bunyip = Australian yeti, or bigfoot.

Burl = give it a try. Use: 'Let's give it a burl.'

Bush = area usually countryside which is away from the city.

Bushranger = Australia's outlaw equivalents to the Northern American folklore cowboys … from the 1800 to early 1900's.

Bush tucker = outback native food.

BYO = bring your own (booze).

Blue in the face = the act of ... repeating something or doing something over and over again.

Blue = fight or argument. Use: Seeing a couple arguing passionately = 'They are having a blue.'

Bogan = socially inept. (rednecks)

Hasn't got a Brass razoo (is penniless). Use: 'He hasn't got a brass razoo!'

Bonza = well done or good job (that job is bonza!)

Booze bus = used by police to capture drunk drivers.

Bottle=o = bottle shop, liquor store. Use: I'm just going to the bottle. Do you need me to grab you anything?'

Brekkie = breakfast. Use: 'what are we having for brekkie?'

Barney Rubble or just barney = Rhyming slang for trouble.

Bull dust = bullshit.

Bush pig = derogatory term used for a female who appears undesirable by any standard.

Budgie smugglers = men's swimming costume.

C

Cactus = dead /in trouble.

Cark it = die. Use: 'How's Brian?'

'Oh! He carked it years ago fighting sharks.'

Captain Cook = rhyming slang for 'take a look'.

'Give it a crack' = have a go at something even if you believe you may not succeed.

Cobber = good friend. Use: 'Everything is good cobber.'

Cask = wine cask.

Cheerio = good bye.

Chock-o-block = full.

Chin wag = to have a good chat.

Chips = French fries.

Choof-off = to go.

Chook = chicken.

Coldie = a cold beer.

Come good = turn out all right.

Corroboree = Aboriginal festival dance.

Cozzie = swimming costume.

Crook = ill, badly made, substandard.

Cuppa = cup of tea.

Cut lunch = sandwiches.

Coldie = beer. Use: Grab us a coldie will ya (you)?'

'Cunning as a dunny (toilet) rat' = an expression for cunning.

Chunder = Throw up or get sick.

Chunder loo = spew... the word 'chunder' originated with the first immigrants to Australia, who suffered from seasickness during the voyage. They'd shout 'Watch out under!' before heaving over the sides on to the decks below.

A cartoon character Chunder Loo of Akim Foo, who appeared in advertisements for a boot polish mob in the Sydney Bulletin in the early 20th Century maybe gave birth to the word.

D

Daks = pants.

Dog and bone = Rhyming slang for phone.

Dinky=di = authentic.

Digger =The rights and acceptance of the 'digger', the 'mate', the 'common man'. Used especially in war setting.

Dag, daggy = mildly abusive term for socially inept person, nerd, nerdy.

Damper = bush loaf made from flour and water, cooked in camp oven.

Deli = delicatessen.

Didgeridoo = tube-shaped wooden Indigenous musical instrument.

Digger = Australian soldier.

Dill = idiot.

Dinky=di = the real thing.

Dob in = to tell on someone.

Docket = receipt, bill.

Dole = unemployment payment.

Don't come the raw prawn = Use: 'Don't 'come the raw prawn' (try and fool me) with that!'

Dunny = toilet.

Dope = silly, stupid, bordering on an idiot. Use: 'That bloke (guy male) is a dope.'

Doin' a Bradbury = winning by virtue of everyone in front of you falling over (courtesy of Australian Olympian Steve Bradbury picking up gold medal in the in the Winter Olympics).

'Down under' = Australia.

'Dead as a maggot' = Dead.

Drongo = no=hoper or fool. Often you may hear it used alongside an expression like = 'Someone whose 'lift doesn't go to the top floor' or whose 'lights are on but no-one's home''. The term Drongo is derived from a racehorse of that name in the 1920s, which never won a race out of 37 starts.

Dropkick = useless person.

Dunny = toilet.

Durri = cigarette.

E

Earbash = talk nonstop.

Esky = Cooler used for keeping drinks and food cold.

Eggxactly = exactly.

Excellent = just great.

F

'Flat out'= working tirelessly. Use: 'How's work?'

Reply: 'Flat out'. Use: 'Flat out like a lizard drinking' (very busy)

Fair go! = chance. Use: 'Give us a fair-go (chance).'

Fairy floss = cotton candy.

Fanny = crude term for female genitalia.

Flat chat, flat out, flat stick = going very fast.

Footy = football.

Full as a boot = drunk.

Funny farm = mental institution.

Fair dinkum= to exclaim a fact or truth in a statement often with some disbelief that the event occurred. Use:' the weather has changed from sunny to 'raining cats and dogs'' (raining heavily). Reply: 'Fair dinkum?'

Frog and toad = Rhyming slang for (road).

'Face like a dropped pie' = a saying for someone who is ugly.

Fit as a Mallee bull = very fit and strong, in good physical condition. The Mallee is a region in Victoria,

South Australia = a parched area where an animal would need to be tough=minded and fit to endure.

Full as a centipede's sock drawer = very full in appetite or packing.

Firies = firefighters.

F*ck me = denoting astonishment. Use: 'the Prime=minister got taken by a shark.' 'Well f*ck me!'

Furphy = a mistruth. A Furphy is a tall tale. It comes from old steel water carts made by the firm 'Furphy and Furphy' back in the 19th century that were used on farms, but were also taken over to the battlefields in WWI. The troops would gather around them to have a drink of water and swap stories/gossip and information that could end up being second, third, or fourth hand and thus wasn't always reliable. Hence, the phrase telling a Furphy was born.

'Full as a boot' or 'full as a state school' = an expression for a full stomach after eating or drinking too much.

Fugly = Fucking ugly. Use: 'That's an ugly painting, swimming pool, dog, cat, picture etc...''

G

Galah = an Australian bird that is loud and not very smart. Use: 'He's carrying on like a flaming galah!'

G'day! = hello. Use = 'G'day mate how's things?'

Going like hot cakes = selling fast.

Garbos = refuse workers.

'Go off like a frog in a sock' = go berserk. Use= 'he's going off like a frog in a sock!'

Goon = cheap boxed wine.

Go troppo = go crazy. Apparently, first termed for people thought to have become a bit odd from the tropical heat in places like Darwin.

Galah = noisy parrot, hence 'noisy idiot'.

Game = brave.

Gander = look: have a gander.

Garbo = person who collects your garbage.

Gas bag = talk a lot.

Give it away = give up.

G'day = good day, traditional Australian greeting.

Good oh = OK.

Good on ya = well done.

Grazier = large=scale sheep or cattle farmer.

Grog = alcohol.

Grizzle = complain.

Grouse = great. Use = 'That steak and beer are grouse!'

H

'Hooroo' = casual good-bye (not commonly said but can be thrown in a conversation. Use = "OK I'm off then!' Reply 'OK. Hooroo!'

Have a root = have sex.

'He needs that like a third armpit'' = he doesn't need it at all.

'He played a Barry' = he did shockingly badly. Barry is short for Barry Crocker and rhymes with shocker. Crocker sang the theme tune for the Australian soap TV show 'Neighbours'.

Hang on a tick = wait a minute. Use: 'Hang on a tick (wait a minute) I will get you that.'

Hoon = idiot, hooligan, loud show-off, over the top rev-head (motor enthusiast).

Hooroo = good bye.

How are ya? = standard greeting = how are you?

How ya going? = how are you doing.

Howzat = asking how something is.

I

'It's gone walkabout' = used when something goes missing or can't be found. Use: 'I don't know where my sunnies are; they've gone walkabout.' Often a term used for indigenous Australians who as Aborigines have spiritual callings and go 'walkabout to realise their identity. Often this may have been done immediately and so if things suddenly go missing then they've gone 'walkabout'.

'I'm stuffed' = an expression meaning, 'I'm full' as in finishing a big meal or 'I am tired' from all the hard work.

Iffy = suspect. Use: 'So you want to trekking into the desert outback at midday? Well that is a bit iffy,' or 'that orange tastes a bit iffy'.

Idiot box = television.

iffy = risky or suspect: something a bit iffy.

J

Jatz crackers = rhyming slang for knackers (testicles).

Jack of it = fed up with it, had enough (of a situation).

Jiffy = short time. Use: 'I shall see you in a jiffy.'

Job you = hit you or punch you. Use: 'keep that up and I'll job you.'

Journo = journalist.

Jumper = sweater.

Jingoes = Amazing. Use: 'Jingoes … that's a good car.'

K

'Kangaroos loose in the top paddock' = eccentric or not very bright. Use: 'He's got few kangaroos loose in the top paddock.'

Keen = very absorbed.

Kiwi = person from New Zealand.

Knickers = underwear.

Knock = criticise, scoff or ridicule.

Knock off work = time to go home.

Knock up = wake up. Use = ' I will knock you up.'

Knackered = Tired. Use: 'I'm knackered.'

L

Legless = someone who is very drunk. Use: 'He is legless.'

'Lolly Water'= a non-boozy beverage e.g. soda and fizzy drinks.

'Littley' = a young one (child).

Lamington = square of sponge cake covered in chocolate icing and   coconut (an Aussie icon).

Lift = elevator.

'Like a madman's jelly' = expression for 'all over the place' or 'messy'.

'Like a shag on a rock' = lonely or exposed. It simply derived from the word for a particular bird. It simply means that you are lonely or exposed, seeing as the regular behaviour of a shag is to stand on a rock with its wings outstretched to dry off after diving for fish. Use = 'Gee, you left me like a shag on a rock!'

Lollies = sweets, candy.

Lurker = a schemer.

M

Manchester = household linen.

Mate = friend, general term of familiarity, whether you know the person or not.

Middy = 285 ml beer glass.

Missus = your wife or partner.

Mobile phone = cellular phone.

Mozzies = mosquitoes.

Maccas = McDonald's restaurant.

Mad as a meat=axe = crazy.

'Mad as a cut snake' = insanely angry.

'May your chooks turn into emus and kick your dunny door down' = a way of wishing someone bad luck.

'Mouth like the bottom of a cocky cage' = a dry mouth, often as a result of heavy drinking and or smoking. (A cocky is a cockatoo.) Use 'My mouth feel like the bottom of a cockie's cage'.

Mexicans = Victorians.

N

'Nasho' = one who in the past had undergoing compulsory military training.

Neck oil = beer.

Nappy = diaper.

Never-Never = mythical, remote, isolated place in the outback.

Nick = steal.

Nick off = go away! get lost!

No hoper = hopeless case.

Nose = on the nose: something stinks.

No worries = she'll be right, that's OK.

'No worries' = eternal optimism: 'No worries mate it will get done!' Simply put it is a positive in a world of negativity!'

'Not within cooee' = an expression meaning 'nowhere within sight as far as the eye can see or 'ear' can hear'. Use: 'He didn't get within cooee of him' in a running race.

'Not the full quid' = an expression denoting someone who is mentally abnormal or stupid.

'Nurse the baby' = expression to 'look after a baby'. REMEMBER, PEOPLE PLEASE DON'T BREAST FEED!

O

'Ochy' = an octopus.

'Off your face' = very drunk.

Ocker = uncultivated, uncultured, boorish Australian.

Off-sider = assistant or partner.

Off the beaten track = on an unused road, in a remote area.

Oldies = parents.

Once over = looking roughly someone or something over, eyeballing or checking it out.

Outback = remote part of the bush, sometimes called back o'Bourke.

Oz = Australia.

Ozzie = Australian.

P

Pash = kiss.

'Popular as a rattle snake in a lucky dip' = unpopular person.

Piss = to urinate.

Pissed = very drunk.

Piss off = get away from me.

Paddock = field.

Pavlova = meringue and cream dessert.

Perve = to gaze with lust.

Pinch = steal.

Piss = beer.

Pissed = sozzled.

Pissed off = irritated.

Piss in your pocket = brown-nose, completely suck-up top someone.

Piss-weak = no good, gutless, useless.

Pom, Pommie = English person.

Pokies = poker machines.

Postie = mail man.

Prang = motor vehicle accident.

Pub = drinking establishment in the form of a hotel.

Pull your head in = mind your own business!

Push bike = bicycle.

Put up or shut up = prove you can do it or keep quiet!

R

Rack off = get away (Use: Instead of saying 'F*ck off ' you say 'Rack off')

Ranga = someone with red hair.

Root rat = derogatory term used for a man who appears undesirable yet professes to sexual conquests.

'Reckon' = 'Really?

Reg grundies = underpants (rhyming slang for undies).

Ripper/cracker = great, fantastic. Use: 'That was a cracker / ripper of a party!'

'Running around like a blue arse fly' = expression meaning doing a lot in a small amount of time.

'That'd be right' = 'I expected that!'

Rafferty's rules = no rules, a mess.

Randy = sexually excited, horny.

Ratbag = friendly term of abuse.

Rapt = delighted, enraptured.

Reckon! = you bet! Absolutely!

Rego = registration: car registration.

Rip off, ripped-off = you have been cheated.

Ripper = good, also: little ripper.

Rip snorter = something that is great.

Root = have sexual intercourse.

Rooted = tired.

Ropable = very angry or bad-tempered.

Rubber = eraser.

Rubbish = deride, tease: to rubbish.

S

Sanga(er) = sandwich. Use: 'Grab us a sanger when you're out?'

Sacked = fired from work.

Salvo = member of the Salvation Army.

Sandshoes = sneakers, joggers.

Scallops = deep-fried potato cake in New South Wales but universal seafood as shellfish somewhere else.

Schooner = large beer glass.

Semi-trailer = big truck.

Session = lengthy period of heavy drinking or sex.

Sheila = woman (can be somewhat derogatory).

'she'll be apples' = 'She'll be right' = no worries, everything will be fine. Use: 'She be all apples in the morning.'

Shonky = untrustworthy, suspicious.

Shoot through = leave in a hurry.

Sus = suspect.

Shout = buy round of drinks, or pay for someone.

Shove off = go away!

Sickie = day off work ill (or lazy and just not bothered to go into work).

Sloppy joe = cotton fleecy-lined sweater.

Smoko = tea break, go and have a cigarette or rest from work activity.

Snag = sausage.

Speedo's = male swimming costume.

Spit the dummy = throw a tantrum.

Stone the Crows = an expression of amazement.

Use: 'Wow look at Uluru?'

Reply: 'Stone the crows!'

Stickybeak = nosey person.

Sticky = nosey. Use: 'I just want to have sticky regarding this home for sale.'

Stir = clown or joke with person.

Strides = trousers.

Strine = conversation with a lot of Aussie slang.

Stubby = small bottle of beer.

Stuffed = very tired, had too much to eat.

Sunbake = sunbathe. To be out in the sun with a view to getting a tan.

Surfies = surfing fanatics.

Show-pony = someone who tries hard to impress with dress or behaviour.

'She'll be right/she'll be apples' = It'll turn out okay. Use: 'Don't worry mate she'll be apples'

Siphon the python = go to the toilet (for males).

Spit the dummy = have a sudden tantrum.

Stoked = excited.

'Shornie' = a shorn sheep

'Saltie'= a saltwater crocodile

'S'arvo'= 'this afternoon'.

Sic = that is unreal. Use: 'that was a sic concert'

Squizz = to have a look. Use: 'We went shopping and had a squizz around.'

Strewth = Exclamation or mild oath. Use: 'Strewth! Get a load of him/her/ that /them or it?'

Stiffy = an erection (also called a Woodie, bar or boner).

Stubby = a small bottle of beer.

I'm stuffed= numerous meaning depending on how it's used for example after eating a big meal and feeling full = 'I'm stuffed!' or being tired = 'I'm stuffed.' or when in trouble = 'I'm stuffed.' (in trouble).

Stunned mullet = shocked. Use: 'He looked at me like a stunned mullet' or 'stop looking like a stunned mullet and get back to work'.

Stone the crows = expression of amazement. Equivalent to the more modern 'strike a light'. 'Stone the crows...' when viewing something amazing or bewildering.

Sand Gropers = Western Australians

T

Thongs = flip-flops.

Take=away food = fast food, to-go food.

Tall poppies = achievers.

Tea = evening meal, dinner.

Tinny = can of beer.

Too right! = absolutely!

Tracks = make tracks: leave to go home

Truckie = truck driver.

True blue = dinkum.

Tucker = food.

Two-pot (middie) screamer = person with low tolerance for alcohol.

Two-up = traditional heads/tails gambling game.

Ta (as in 'tar') = thankyou.

Tall poppy syndrome= a tendency to think ill of or criticise people simply because they are successful.

Tea= dinner. Use 'Do you want to go out for tea tomorrow?'

'Too right' = 'that's correct'.

Tucker = food.

'Trammie' = a tram driver or conductor.

'True blue' = dinky di (pronounced 'dinky dye') = real or authentic.

U

'Up and down like a bride's nightie' / 'up and down like a dunny seat' = changing your opinion, or overactive.

'Up the duff ' = pregnant.

Up the bush = in the country side.

Up the line = in the countryside.

Up yourself = stuck up or love yourself to death = have a high opinion of yourself.

Ute = pick=up truck (literally a shortening of 'utility').

Uni = university.

Up yourself

V

Vindaloo = rhyming slang for 'spew'.

Vegies = vegetables.

Verbal diarrhoea = talking non=stop, usually nonsense.

W

Wally = silly person. Use: 'Stop carrying on like a wally.'

Woop-Woop = made=up name for a small, unimportant town away in the middle of nowhere. Use: 'He lives way out in Woop- Woop. I'm not driving that far!)

Wag = to skip school or work: to wag school.

Walkabout = lengthy walk away from it all.

Weatherboard = wooden house.

Wharfie = dock worker.

Whinge = complain, moan.

Wobbly = disturbing, unpredictable behaviour, temper tantrum. Use: 'don't chuck a wobbly because you didn't get your own way.'

Wog = derogatory term for foreigner.

Wowser = spoilsport, puritan, old-fashioned.

Write-off = car involved in a crash that is not worth repairing.

Y

Ya = you.

Youse = you.

Yabbie = minor freshwater crayfish.

Yacking = talking non-stop.

Yap = continued talk.

Yahoo = raucous and disruptive person. Use: 'Stop being a yahoo and settle down.'

Yakka = effort. Use: 'Gee that was hard yakka working on those plumbing pipes.'

Yobbo = uncouth, aggressive person.

Yonks = ages, an extended time. Use: 'She can talk for yonks' or I haven't seen you for yonks.'

Z

Zonked = too exhausted to concentrate on something physical or mental. Use: 'I'm really zonked from that.'

Zebra crossing = painted pedestrian crossing on the street.

3

'WHOAH, slow down!'...

I hear you say?

Modern Trends

How often do you get muddled and mixed up with how Australians make words rhyme? How often do you listen to words that seemingly just disappear mid-sentence like the speaker forgot the last part of the word existed?

It often appears Australians use language that rhymes. Additionally, Australians abbreviate words to apparently save both their breath and energy. But one isn't holding back father time when using 'frog n toad' instead of 'road' or saying 'brekkie' instead of 'breakfast' are they? Perhaps the Aussie is best known for the above choice of language in order to less formalise speech and smooth the conversation over.

Whereas Aussies over 50 years of age tend to use slang with 'o' endings (muso, smoko) or rhyming slang like 'pig's ear' for 'beer' or many proverbs the younger generation (some 30 years down to the early teens (12 13 years etc...) a few twists and turns to the vocabulary:

Dope as F#ck = good.

AF = As f#ck.

Lit = good.

Resurrection = nothing.

Chat = foul or disgusting.

Awko = awkward.

Cheddar = money.

Gucci = cool.

Salty = resentful or irritated.

Straight fire = baking hot / fashionable.

Bae = before anyone else. Use: 'You are bae baby!'

Snack = Attractive.

Thick = looking good in your skin no matter what size you are male or female.

Keeper = one for later.

Cut =damaged in a sexual way = slut or root rat.

... and countless more.

Commonly, modern trends are to chop the ends off words (uni for university) and affix an 's' to the first language unit or syllable 'totally' unacceptable becomes 'totes' unacceptable.

But this is a modern linguistic attitude not an 'I couldn't give shit' attitude.

While Australians might think they speak standard English, newly arrived migrants often struggle with the unusual colloquialisms that make up everyday speech.

Irony and sarcasm come a lot into play when speaking 'Australian'. For instance, Australians like to pose a statement as a question like 'how good is this weather?' = and the unsuspecting think that they have to provide an answer.

A further example is: 'What about (insert sports team, the prime minister or favourite actor?) How good is he/she going?'

Then come the head scratches. But that is just one way of how Australian's communicate.

That said, Australians do make a habit to shorten words and somewhat get one's brain firing when one has to interpret.

What's ta?'

Ta (pronounced 'tar' as in car) is thanks.

Often Australians leave out the beginning of sentences for example: 'Can you please' or 'can you get' becomes 'grab us a tinny (Beer).' And when retrieved it is welcomed with a ta (thanks).

Aussies speak English but it is quite different from other tongue and way of talking, and the most important thing for many people is to learn the slang word and to understand the intention of the conversation and also to master when something is a joke or not even when humour is used to disarm probable harmful or disappointing events.

Strewth you wouldn't read about it unless you read about it!

The use of =o or ie even o's or 'ty' at the end of a word help to disarm a seriousness and invite informality which often precedes openness and participation. For example:

- Shortie = something / one small and edible.

- 'Saltie' = a saltwater crocodile

- 'Trammie' = a tram driver or conductor.

- 'Ochy' = an octopus.

- Truckie = truck driver.

- 'S'arvo' = this afternoon.

And even nicknames for Prime ministers e.g. Sco-Mo = Scott Morrison.

STREWTH - HOW TO BE AN AUSSIE IN 10 MINUTES

4

HOW TO SPEAK LIKE AN AUSSIE!!!

PRONOUNCING WORDS IN 'AUSTRALIAN ' in 12 EASY WAYS

Like any other country, there are a variety of accents and differences across Australia, but a few simple tricks can help you master a gentle, general Aussie accent to start with.

1

LISTEN

Listen when an Aussie speaks. Take in their accents. The most remarkably repeated Australian way of speaking uses movements whether that be body or facial and can be as animated or inanimate through a broken, untidy, often informal or laid-back approach.

69 | P a g e

There is a common mouthful approach to eating then spewing out the words like stuffing your mouth full of food then jettisoning it in one go.

The best way to learn this is to just hang with an Aussie and listen and watch. And often they do and say it fast.

For example: 'Good day mate, having a good one?' comes out as 'G'day mate avvin good=one'

As your ears prick=up mentally jot down some bits and pieces about how they talk:

For instances, what do you hear which is familiar with each word or sentence spoken? Focus on their use of a.e.i.o.u.

Most Australian accents are more relaxed then imagined. They aren't people shooting off words faster than Yosemite Sam fires bullets from his gun or a person who 's words come out so slow they need to punch them to the ground rather an in=between mix.

In fact, Australians and their accents developed from colonists originating from all round England but namely southern England. As such, it is closely related to the modern English language or Londoner accent, but with a twist and slightly more 'coherent'.

2

PITCH and VOCALISE

Keep your pitch and vocalising steady, quick, and soft as if saying something in one sentence. Additionally, say this in monotone. The next sentence you may raise or lower an octave but each sentence almost needs to be distinctively familiar as each word is pronounced. Picture a steam train leaving a tunnel and comprised of carriages (words) all connected. Here we deliver a sentence similar; leaving the tunnel in almost one move (breath). So, it is important to keep the tongue almost petrified or glued to the bottom of your mouth. Now deliver the statement!

In deconstructing sentences and pronunciation let's start with using the 'i's in words to sound like the 'oi' as in 'oil. So, five becomes f oi ve. Remember don't make it so loud and in your face rather a subtle pronunciation. He is alive becomes he is 'al oi ve.' That is tripe become that is 'tr oi pe', write become 'wr=oi te' and like becomes 'l=oi=ke.' But note keep it subtle even rising tone on your 'i' pitch ever so slightly. 1234567891011

3

THE QUICK A's

Turn your awkward A sound into something you say when using the word 'plate'. However, say it faster. 'p...l...a...t...e' becomes 'plate', 'w...a...y becomes way.. 'p..l..a...y..' becomes play, 's...t...a...t...e becomes a rapid fire state.

Use: 'how was your d...a...y?' becomes 'howwasyourday?'

4

DISTINCTION

For every A sound that exists in the words cat, hat, mat, sat and rat pronounce the letter 'a' as in 'heh' or eh'. Remember soft, subtle, very quick and distinct.

Mat = M...eh ...t.

Rat = R... eh...t.

Plat = Pl... eh...t.

Use: 'Did you Pl..eh...t your hair on the m..eh...t?'

becomes (quickly), 'Did you Pl..eh...t ' your hair anthem..eh...t?'[1234567891011]

5

'T' GOES TO 'D' AT THE END OF A WORD

Cut 't's' and replace with a subtle sounding 'd' at the END of words.

'Have you got it?' becomes 'have you goddid?'

At the beginning pronounce t's but slacken off as the word finishes almost forgetting to end the word for e.g. Tomorrow becomes tommorr. Use: 'Are you still going tommorr?'

The sound is the tiny, distinct stop you make between the two sounds, like someone has made the last part of the world disappear. When you say the word, 'slight,' you want to sound more like 'sl=ide.' Use: 'Her build is only slight' becomes 'Her build is only slide' but dismiss the d. 'Right' becomes 'ride' without the d. This is perfected by simply not touching your tongue to the roof of your mouth when perfect 'ts are meant to be formed.

'This is called a glottal stop and is common around the word in many languages.' 1234567891011

6

CANCEL THE LENGTHY 'R' SOUND FROM THE END OF WORDS

Cancel the lengthy R sound from the end of words and like rubber and replace it with an 'ah.' For example, instead of 'rubber,' you would say 'rubb...ah.' Instead of 'car,' you'd say 'c...ah.' 'pleasure' becomes ' pleas...ah', 'beer' becomes 'bee (ah)' without the roll of the 'r'.[1234567891011]

7

MAKE YOUR STATEMENTS SOUND MORE LIKE QUESTIONS

How good is Ian Thorpe swimming?

How bad is our prime minister?

What about those sharks?

What about my pants?

Do you reckon he could go any slower?

What about the way she drinks a beer?

How good is that?

8

GET RID OF THE ENDING FROM A WORD WHEN IT FINISHES WITH 'G'

Most Aussies have never heard of the letter 'g' at the end of their words 'g' so snip off the G from any '=ing' ending word.

Singing becomes singin'

Fishing becomes fishin'

Rooting becomes rootin'

Running becomes runnin'

Fucking becomes fucken'

Selling becomes sellin'

9

USE AUSTRALIAN TELEVISION, MOVIES, AND MUSIC TO PICK UP SLANG

End phrases with the word 'mate.'

Mate can be used anytime you would normally say 'guys,' 'man' (as in, 'come on, man/ guys/ mate!'), or similarly simple slang terms for a person.

Use 'Reckon' when you're thinking of something. 'I reckon that's not a bad idea, mate.'

Throwing in the phrase 'she'll be 'apples,' and then 'sweet' to ease concerns. 'I hope I didn't burn dinner... Ah, she'll be apples, sweet mate.'

'Yeh right mate sweet!'

10

AUSSIE SLANG TENDS TO USE METAPHORS IN SPEECH

If you're an accomplished impressionist, try this:

'Runnin' around like a blue arse fly'

'She's got more hide then a buffalo!'

'Last time I saw a mouth like that it had a hook in it!'

'He's got a head bigger than Uluru!'

'He's fitter than a Mallee-bull.'

'He's got ahead like a dropped pie.'

'He's as useful as car salesman in the desert.'

Also pay close attention to the variation / nuance / inflection used in Australian speech. It is often greatly magnified.

Australians typically use a lot of facial and body movements when speaking; their mouths switch from side to side accompanied with plenty of hand gestures and even eyebrow movement.

11

PLAY WITH YOUR WORDS LIKE A BABY A RATTLE

Develop a soft, playful, and twangy tone of voice. Speak through your nose making sounds appear 'nasally'. Read magazines and newspapers out loud. Aussie accents have personality, so add a playful and happy tone when speaking. Just like in any other country, there are multiple accents and ways of speaking, so listening to Australian speakers in any capacity possible = TV, net, movies, music and news.

12

SELF-CONFIDENCE IS CLEAR IN COLLOQUIAL LANGUAGE

Whether Colloquial language is boisterous ('av' a go ya mug') and cheeky ('up the duff ') or loud 'Stop IT YOU FLAMIN GALAH' and direct 'Mate, pull your finger out!' (work harder), it is always confidently said.

Maybe the Australian community is where their confidence / resilience stems from. When things get tough or feels down and out like all hope is lost Aussies come collectively as one. Australian humour is ironic, self-mocking, and now and again rough-cut. They/We make light of ourselves and the hard times.

Australians look to abbreviate as much as possible. 'Aussie' is a perfect example. Perhaps Australians shorten their words because it softens our rough edges, confronting accent, and easy-going ways. Either way, you know you're Australian when 'you believe that the more you shorten someone's name the more you like them.'

Here are some commonly used abbreviations in the Australian vernacular:

Farnsy (John Farnham)

Blowie (blowfly)

Mozzie (mosquito)

Totes (totally)

Cocky (cockroach or cockatoo)

Bushie (bushman)

Veggies (vegetables)

Chewie (chewing gum)

Bikkies (biscuits)

Chrissie (Christmas)

Avo (avocado)

Cozzie (swimming costume)

Snags (sausages)

Sickie (a day off sick from work)

Salvos (Salvation Army)

Beaut (beauty, beautiful)

Uggies (Ugg boots)

Mozzie (mosquito)

Servo (Service Station)

Smoko (small break)

Indies (independent)

Some words just get changed, for example:

Lift = Elevator

Thongs =Sandals

Tuck Shop = Canteen, Kiosk, Cafeteria

Footpath = Sidewalk

Bonnet = Hood of car

Boot = Trunk of car

Ute = Truck

Servo = Gas station

Petrol = gas

Nappy = Diaper

Dummy = Pacifier

Super Market = Grocery Store

Carpark = Parking lot

Jumper = Sweater

Soft Drink = Soda

Lollies = Candy

Ciggies = Smokes

Trolley = Tram or Shopping cart depending where you are and what you are on

Tomato Sauce = Ketchup

Biscuit = Cookie

Scone = American Biscuit

Jocks = Underwear

Rubber = Eraser

Rubber = French letter or condom

Fanny = Vagina

Tap = Faucet

Wind = Bowel Gas

Petrol = Gas

Rubbish Bin = Trash Can

Stoked = Really happy

Sheila = Woman

Prawn = Shrimp

Stubby = Beer

Rat Bags=Naughty Kids

Biscuits = Cookies

REMEMBER, that there's more to an Australian accent than just saying, 'mate' all the time. Learning anything is work. And if you're good, and can put in some slang it adds to the colour especially if you're trying to be convincing.

Australians will respect you if you can do a convincing Aussie accent, but will ridicule you if you do a poor one. Take it all in your stride. Australian accents are notoriously hard for non-Australians to pick up. An Australian will instantly spot a 'fake' accent, and will likely laugh at you.

It's best not to try and mimic the indigenous-Australian accent.

The Sun sets in the Outback

STONE THE CROWS!

Australians are as incomparable as they come. From their attire sense, custom and jargon they have you commonly scratching your head to work them out. They like to use humour to criticise and ridicule others and themselves but all in good nature.

Moreover, Aussies like to believe they are warm, giving and friendly and want you to embrace their way of life.

So ...

Cobber (my good Mate), settle down. You just need to grab a sanga (sandwich) or sausage sizzle (butcher's sausage on a bread roll), wash it down with some neck oil (alcohol) and chillax (chill out /relax). It's no use rushing on the tucker (food) as you don't want to chunder (vomit). And remember to go easy on the three cheers (beers) you don't want to look like a wally (silly person) if you over indulge.

Firstly, to understand a little bit of the why and what for of the Aussie way of doing things you probably need to consider some relaxation time. So, here's an idea ... why not now head down to the beach to watch the world go by? But watch=out for the after darks (rhyming slang for 'sharks')! It will probably be a beaut arvo with an optic nerve (rhyming slang for 'perve') or two as the good bodies walk on by. Don't forget your thongs (sandals) it's Summer and it is hot out. Blokes don't forget the budgie smugglers (swimmers). Now, lay out the farmer's plough (rhyming slang for 'towel') and take it all in.

You know, up the line (in the countryside) they don't get much time to do this but when they get a chance to hit the big smoke their brains run amok looking at what city folk get up to.

Unless you have a few kangaroos loose in the top paddock (not there mentally) there is no way you wouldn't enjoy down under with all the scenery (and the beach is just one type). There is heaps more. Hit the frog and toad (rhyming slang for 'road'), go out west, or hit the bush (the countryside) and simply people watch, take in some adventures and abuse the climate ... and you can't lose.

But hold onto your nuts (don't panic). You will soon realise that Australians are unique. Although you may encounter a few bogans(rednecks) and tall poppy's (overly confident people) overall the chance to blend in with people from ambos(ambulance persons) and garbos(refuse workers) to musos(musicians) and poli's (politicians) will delight you especially when you realise there's a whole new world out there (right here) and full of colourful language to boot. But hold on don't spit the dummy (have a tantrum) with what lay ahead, please don't go off like frog in a sock(berserk). Fair dinkum(truly) it's not an insurmountable task to take it all in. You have plenty of time to learn the lingo and understand the Australian way of life!

So, what I'm saying is give me just some of your reason and rhyme (rhyming slang for 'time') and we can solve the dilemma.

ENJOY AUSTRALIA!

BOOKS BY

BILL SCRATCH CUNNINGHAM

1. How to Get Rid of Mosquitoes (MOZZIES) ... NOW!

2. How to be an AUSSIE in 10 minutes!!! All the Words, Sayings and Aussie Stuff to Fill your Boots!

3. How to GET RID of FLEAS, Ants, Mice and RATS ... INSTANTLY!

4. How to Control your Puppy / Dog Now ...

100 Excellent Dog tips YOU MUST KNOW!

5. How to Get rid of Cockroaches... IMMEDIATELY!

About the Author

Bill 'Scratch' Cunningham has lived in Australia all his life – outback Australia that is. He has been a bush expert for over 40 years extending his research into 'Australianisms'. He has a fascination in natural flora and fauna and solving the most obstinate of problems facing human beings with simple but powerful solutions from all thing's pests to pets.

References

1. Ockerisms locally written 2019

2. Interviews with local Australians Bill Cunningham

3. Australia local identities Bill Cunningham

4. Mentalfloss.com/article/52789/how-do-Australian-accent

5. Theguardian.com/commentisfree/2015/Apr./30/ glottal-stop

6. Felixexi.com/how-to-speak-with-an-australian-accent-for-american-dummies/

7. bbc.com/news/magazine=28708526

Mentalfloss.com/article/61847/25-awesome-australian-slang-terms

8. bbc.com/news/magazine-27888329

9. Aussie-info worldatlas.com

10. Abc.net why Australian slang is not dying. Australian pronunciation internet.

11. Wikihow.com/index.title-Speak-with-an-Australian-Accent&action.

abc wikipaedia

Printed in Great Britain
by Amazon

20623999R00058